Dare to Dream

Dare to Dream

Verbal Remedies™ to light you up and set you free

by Breah Parker

SOURCEBOOKS, INC.®
NAPERVILLE, ILLINOIS

Published by Sourcebooks, Inc.
P.O. Box 4410, Naperville, Illinois 60567-4410
(630) 961-3900
FAX: (630) 961-2168

Library of Congress Cataloging-in-Publication Data

Parker, Breah.
Dare to dream: verbal remedies to light you up and set you free / by Breah Parker.
p. cm.
ISBN 1-57071-507-6 (alk. paper)
1. Self-actualization (Psychology) I. Title.

BF637.S4 P355 2001
158—dc21

00-066167

Printed and bound in the United States of America

CPI 10 9 8 7 6 5 4 3 2 1

This Book is Dedicated To My **Incredible** Children, **Ryan, Paige** and **Taylre!**

Be Who You Are...

It's More Than

Enough!

Figuring out who to thank for helping to make this book a reality was a daunting task. Where do I begin, where do I stop? So many people, so little space. I'd like to start at the very beginning and thank Lorraine and Frank, my Mom and Dad... Bob and Kathi, my bro' and sis... Scott, the man I grew up with... Ryan, Paige and Tayler, my kids... Uncle Joe and Aunt Peg, who first told me I was a writer... Lisa Clare Shannon and Georgette Braadt, who "womanned" the Surtex booth... Deb Werksman, my editor, who made sure I wrote this book... Megan Dempster, who made sure this book got to press... Pripo Teplitsky, my friend, mentor and my inspiration in the final stages... Zander Teplitsky, who brought sunshine to my studio... Rainbow Teplitsky, who shared her boys, her love, and her magic... Dylan McCarthy, whose gentle spirit calmed me down... Althea Matthews, who helped make sense of my space and head... Fou and Chloe, my puppies, who warmed my heart and my feet as I wrote and colored the pages... Carole Lacy for providing a beautiful place to work... Kerry Canfield, for staying late so I could make my deadline... and the many friends and family who have been teachers and inspiration. I am grateful for the presence of all of you.

Table of Contents

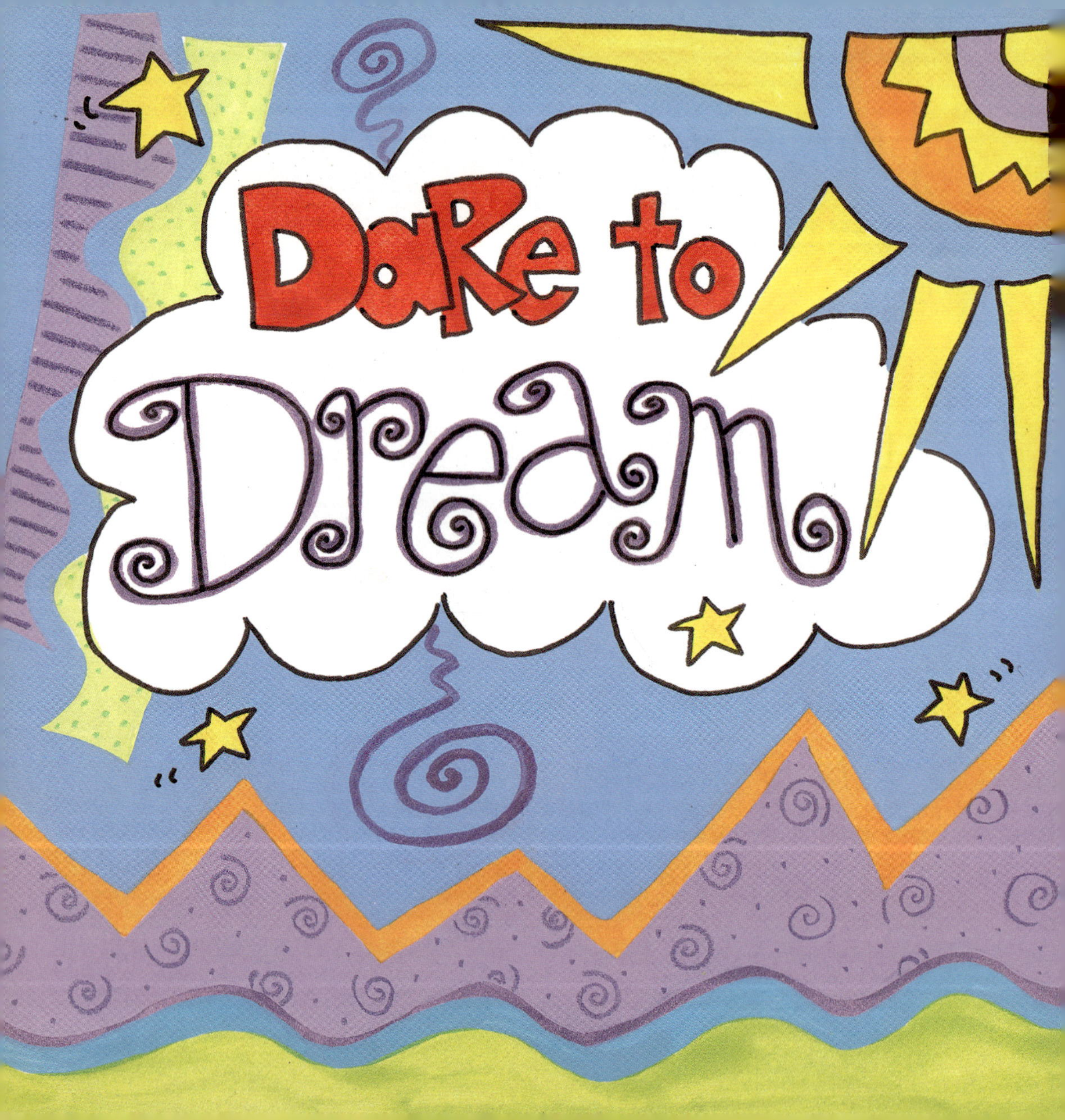
Dare to
Dream

Dare to Dream

Dare to dream! Dream wildly, dream with courage, and with the belief that you can make your dreams come true!

When you believe in your dreams, you give them the power to manifest in your life, to become real.

A few years ago in Paris, I sat in on a rehearsal session for the band in which my dear friend (I call him my "French Son") Alban plays the saxophone. He and the band were

Fantastique!

Al had been learning to play the sax when he lived with me and my family while he was in high school. It was clear back then how much

He Loved his music

and even more evident as I listened and watched him with the band.

Afterward, he expressed his frustration that he could not make a living playing his sax.

I encouraged him to try, telling him...

"We can do whatever we want to do in our lives if we simply believe in ourselves and work at it. Everything is possible."

Everything
and ALL is
POSSIBLE!

Alban, youthful and somewhat skeptical, spiritedly asked if I was doing what I wanted to do in this life. Was I "doing my dream"?

I gulped, took a deep breath, and admitted to him and to myself that I wasn't. My dream was to create a cartoon character who would be **a voice of optimism** and **humor**, a voice of **inspiration**. I'd been too afraid, felt unworthy, too busy, etc. Lots of excuses, no good reasons.

I sounded like a new age hypocrite and that felt bad. Alban, or anyone, would only believe my ever-so-optimistic philosophy if I could **MAKE MY OWN DREAMS A REALITY.**

Dreams of Adventure and Achievement

Dreams of Discovery and Enlightenment

DREAMS OF Romance AND LOVE

Dreams

of creation and

inspiration

“Dreams of JOY And PEACE”

BIG
and
TECHNICOLOR
and
Little
PRIVATE
Dreams.

Conscious dreams
and unconscious dreams...

HIGHER

Consciousness dreams.

I knew I was stuck. I had to prove my words with **ACTION**. My message in giving up my dreams would always speak more loudly and clearly than anything I could utter. That is a **VERY BIG LESSON** I learned... action really does speak louder and in more volume than any series of words ever could. The words are important reminders, guidelines for living...

VERBAL REMEDIES

For the soul.

Action is living proof of the words we speak, and the strongest teaching tool we have in this human existence.

Action Speaks
the loudest
and ClearesT
messages

The Creation of
Spirit...

SOUL speaking to BODY

BODY speaking to SOUL

Lessons played back,

Remembrances

of the

Light

SYMBOLS of what is YET to BE.

I left Paris with the determination to

begin the **JOURNEY**

of daring to live my dream. What had seemed to be a far-fetched idea, began to come into focus. By making the commitment to my dream, I began to take the steps to

Make iT happen.

The "female cartoon character" became

Lorelie, the inspirational cartoon character!

All along the way, I was given little gifts and big ones in the form of suggestions and also inspirations through friends, family, and strangers. One gift came in the form of a new friend and his suggestion to put together a web site...

www.Verbalremedies.com

Sometimes the gifts didn't feel like gifts at all, rather they seemed like very painful and unnecessary lessons. Of course, as I have learned, **every lesson is** part of the path and a **necessary** one. Over time, it became obvious that everything happens for a

Reason.

Trust that Everything Happens for a very good Reason!

There is a lesson to be learned within every situation. Sometimes the reasons and the lessons are difficult to see, but with a little extra attention, they become CLEAR. I learned to believe in myself, my abilities, my dreams, and a UNIVERSAL PLAN. Knowing that a particularly uncomfortable situation offers a valuable learning tool somewhere WITHIN makes even the toughest times tolerable. That knowledge provides me with Strength to keep wading through. The sound of sucking mud as I pick up one foot after the other becomes a source of pride and Evidence of movement.

Create
A
Sacred
Space

Create a Sacred Space

Living your dreams provides an unimaginable Freedom of Spirit. Having freedom of spirit comes through finding peace inside your soul. Peace inside finds its way through to the space you live in.

But how can you Find Peace in a world where you have so little control? Good news... you don't have to... Peace Finds You.

Trying to hold on to the pieces of peace you can recognize and feel safe with becomes stressful, creating less peace in the effort. Time and tasks accomplished becomes the critical measure of self. "How much did I get done during the allotted time?"

A quieting of all the voices of "should... must... ...gotta..." will alleviate the CRAZIES created by this type of thinking. So it is important to create a sacred SPACE to quiet the MIND.

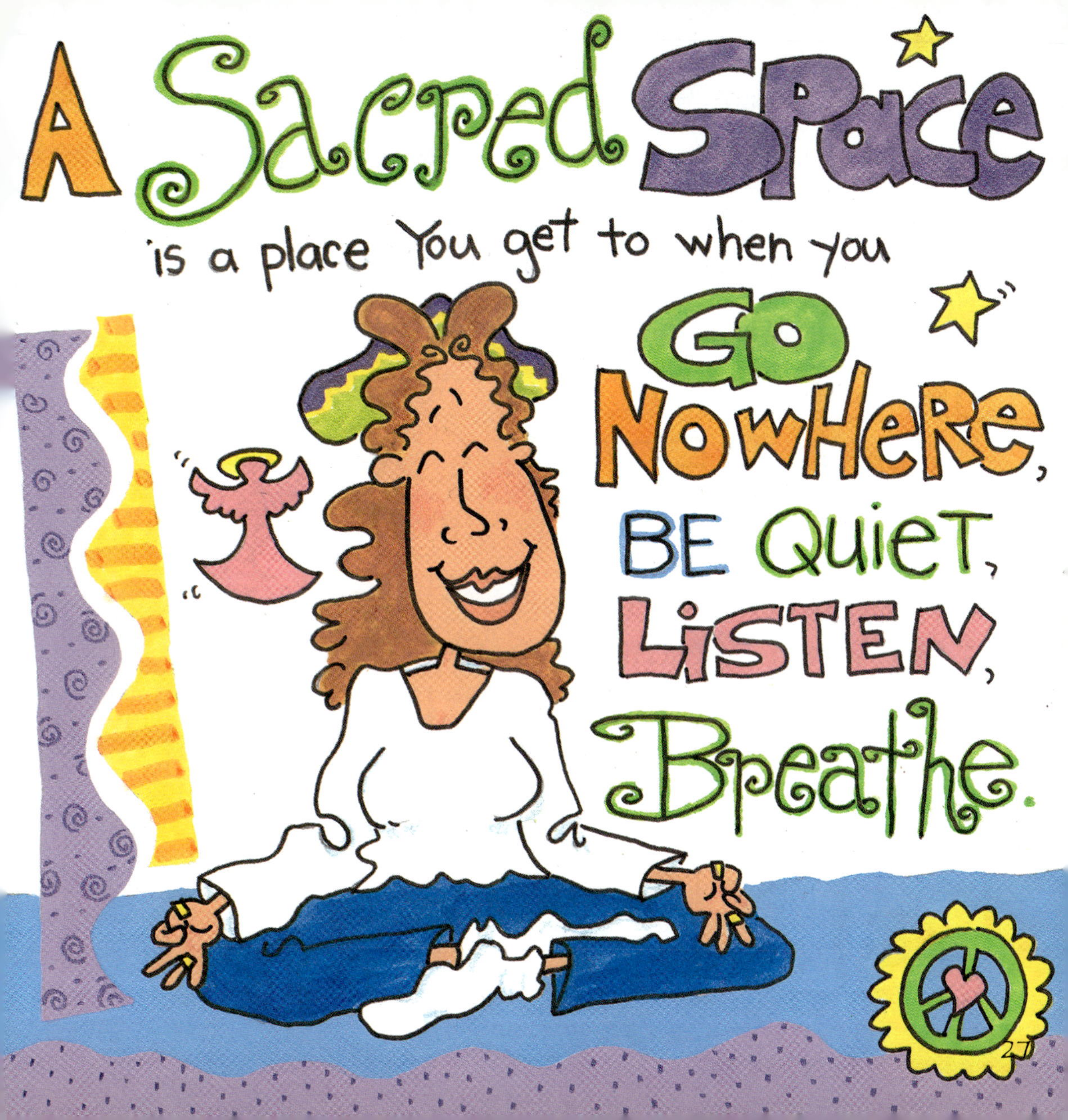
A Sacred Space
is a place You get to when you
GO
NoWHeRe,
BE QuieT,
LiSTEN,
Breathe.

Create your sacred space by MEDITATING, EXERCISING, conscious BREATHING, PLAYING, PAINTING, or whatever produces that feel-good place of contentment. CONTENTMENT is the first step to experiencing PEACE. QUIETING is the first step to experiencing contentment. Take time to be quiet... quiet from the top of your head to the tips of your toes, to the DEEP DOWN WITHIN.

Breathe.

Feel your skin breathe, feel Your blood flow, Feel Your heart beat. Feel the energy of the Earth flow up and through your entire body. Feel the PEACE of the UNIVERSE warm you up inside.

Learning to find that sacred space was particularly difficult for me. I didn't seem able to stop the chatter in my head. I would sit down, cross my legs, open my hands into a "meditation pose" and proceed to think about everything I had to do that day. I just couldn't

GET QUIET.

I asked for help from whoever and whatever might be out there listening. Help came in the form of

Gina Rose.

Gina is an intuitive counselor and spiritual advisor I met years ago in Boulder. (She now lives in the island paradise land of Hawaii!) Gina's insight amazes and enlightens me every time we speak. She has provided some very valuable tools for

SPIRITUAL GROWTH and one of

them is this meditation, that I have personalized a bit and will now share with you...

with Gina's permission.

Find a Quiet place,

one where you won't be disturbed by the telephone or other distractions.

Sit with your Feet touching the Ground in some way, either on a chair (Gina's preferred method) or cross-legged on the floor (which is my preferred method). It helps to have a cushion or pillow tucked right under the base of the spine for Support.

"It's important to keep your SPINE STRAIGHT so there is good ENERGY FLOW.

PICTURE A STRING attached from somewhere out in the stars to the top of your head that holds you Straight and STRONG. If you find yourself slouching, imagine getting a GENTLE little TUG to pull you up..."

Once in position, close your eyes
and begin to

Take deep cleansing Breaths.

Breathe in through your nose, filling
your abdomen, then stomach, then chest...
Hold for a **Few Seconds**
and then blow it all out through your mouth
until you have to gasp for another
breath to fill you back up.

After a few of these breaths, let your breathing come back to a normal and comfortable pace. Now...

Imagine a **LONG CORD** descending from the base of your spine, dropping into the Earth and hooking itself up to the core of the planet. This is your **GROUNDING CORD** and can be anything you like that helps you to feel securely fastened to good old **MOTHER EARTH**.

"Gina suggested a silver thread-like grounding cord, but I use an anchor chain! As it drops I imagine I can hear the sound of the chain links unravelling. Of course, at the end of the chain is a mighty anchor that keeps me very firmly attached!

The next thing is to imagine all your **WORRIES** and **PROBLEMS** **FLOWING DOWN** the cord and **DISPERSING DEEP INTO THE GROUND.** There is no need to enumerate each and every issue, just know they are **LEAVING YOU**."

As they leave, there is now ROOM FOR NEW ENERGY from the Earth to flow up and into your body. TRACE THE ENERGY as though it is a warm and BRIGHT current of LIGHT... traveling from your toes all the way up into your abdomen, about three inches below your navel. This is your

Second Chakra.

When the ENERGY reaches your second chakra, let it flow once again down through the grounding cord into the Earth and again UP THROUGH YOUR TOES, up into your second chakra, creating a REPETITIVE CIRCLE of ENERGY FLOW. Do this for several minutes until you feel satisfied to move on. NEXT, imagine a HALO of GOLD LIGHT six inches above your head.

In that halo of golden light, place a **PICTURE** of what you would **LIKE TO MANIFEST** in your life. Once satisfied with the **VISION** you have created, let the golden light break into hundreds of tiny gold balls that begin dropping into your body through the top of your head.

FILL YOUR BODY starting at your toes, going all the way up to your shoulders, out through your arms and into your fingertips.

Fill your neck and head, letting the little gold balls of light overflow through the top of your head like a **SHOWER** OF **GOLDEN Energy.**

Finish your meditation by taking a deep cleansing breath, holding it, and releasing it slowly through your mouth.

Honor Yourself for giving yourself these precious, quiet moments and...

Sit in The Peace of The Moment.

Leap into Life!

Leap into Life!

Imagine yourself a celestial being, sitting around the **celestial** roundtable with other **angelic** buddies, outlining the **PLAN** for this time around.

"This time you'll be my mother…I'll be your sister…You'll be the one who teaches me **The BIG LESSON** … and you'll be my dog when I finally leave home and need a smiling face and wagging tail to start and end my day."

You then proceed to detail just how you will recognize each other, what lessons you'll teach, wish each other the **Grace** of God (heavenly term for "break a leg") and...

"Leap into Life!"

One by one, we incarnate into Earth school. What better metaphor for leaping into life than the birth of a child? Once committed to heading down the birth canal, nothing stops that burst into the world, accompanied by the sounds of JOY and EXCITEMENT, energy that can hardly contain itself.

Life begins, if we are lucky enough, with every need being met, with Comfort, warmth, and SECURITY... surrounded by

Peace and Love

Surround yourself with peace and love...

The lessons begin.
PEACE and LOVE,
Turbulence and Pain.
Where there is LIGHT
There is dark.
Where there is dark
There is Light.

You have the ability to

CREATE MORE LIGHT

than dark, and, believe me, I know it doesn't feel that way a lot of the time. In the process of living on this planet, you may sometimes get lost, forgetting exactly why you took this

"LEAP"

... maybe even forgetting that you took it

with a purpose.

Yet, there is that NAGGING LITTLE VOICE constantly nudging and prodding, reminding you of a higher purpose, creating a feeling of

"There's just **Something I have To DO**."

Because this is a FREE-WiLL PLANET, it is YOUR CHOICE to listen or not, TAKE ACTION or pass. But you must

Make a choice and...

Exercise
Free
Will!

There are no hard and fast rules for living this life, although there is definitely a PURPOSE FOR your BEING here. How you achieve that purpose is completely UP TO YOU.

That is free will, and it is our gift as humans.

Take Time
for a Little
PEACE
and
Quiet.

Take Time...

What stops you from taking that

"Leap into Life!"...

Finding and taking that simple or great

idea and Making it Happen?

Maybe it is that much denied, but obvious fear of failure... or the not-so-obvious fear of Success.

Let your nagging little voice dare you to

take a good LONG SIGH.

Think about that **ONE THING** that keeps popping up in your thoughts, in your **day dreams**, in your **sleep dreams.**

Breathe.

Close your eyes.

Listen.

What "JUMPS in or crawls in and whispers your name?"

A reminder of somewhere and something...

Is it BIG, is it small,

OR NOTHING AT ALL

But a BREEZE

Drifting in from the

LIGHT?

Is it WARM, is it COLD,
OR NOTHING AT ALL
But a RUSH and a CHILL
through your chest?

Is it NEAR ... is it FAR
OR NOWHERE AT ALL
But the place in the
HEART OF YOUR
SOUL?

Higher consciousness dreaming, through meditation or sleep, sends messages to the body. Spirit provides this tool to access our higher selves, helping to achieve and maintain balance in this human/spiritual existence. Dreams give us a remembrance of the light, which is our source and symbolizes what is yet to come.

Day dreams, sleep dreams, or meditatively induced dreams are sent out into the universal consciousness. It may take a little while to come back around or just seconds, so...

Create Your Dreams and Trust.

"Remember Your Dream"

and work toward it, one step at a time, fully conscious of each step as you take it.

Enjoy the Process

of moving in the direction of your dream.

Trust in your ability to create through dreams and in the patience to let them return to you.

"And in the meantime, Have FUN and Enjoy Life!"

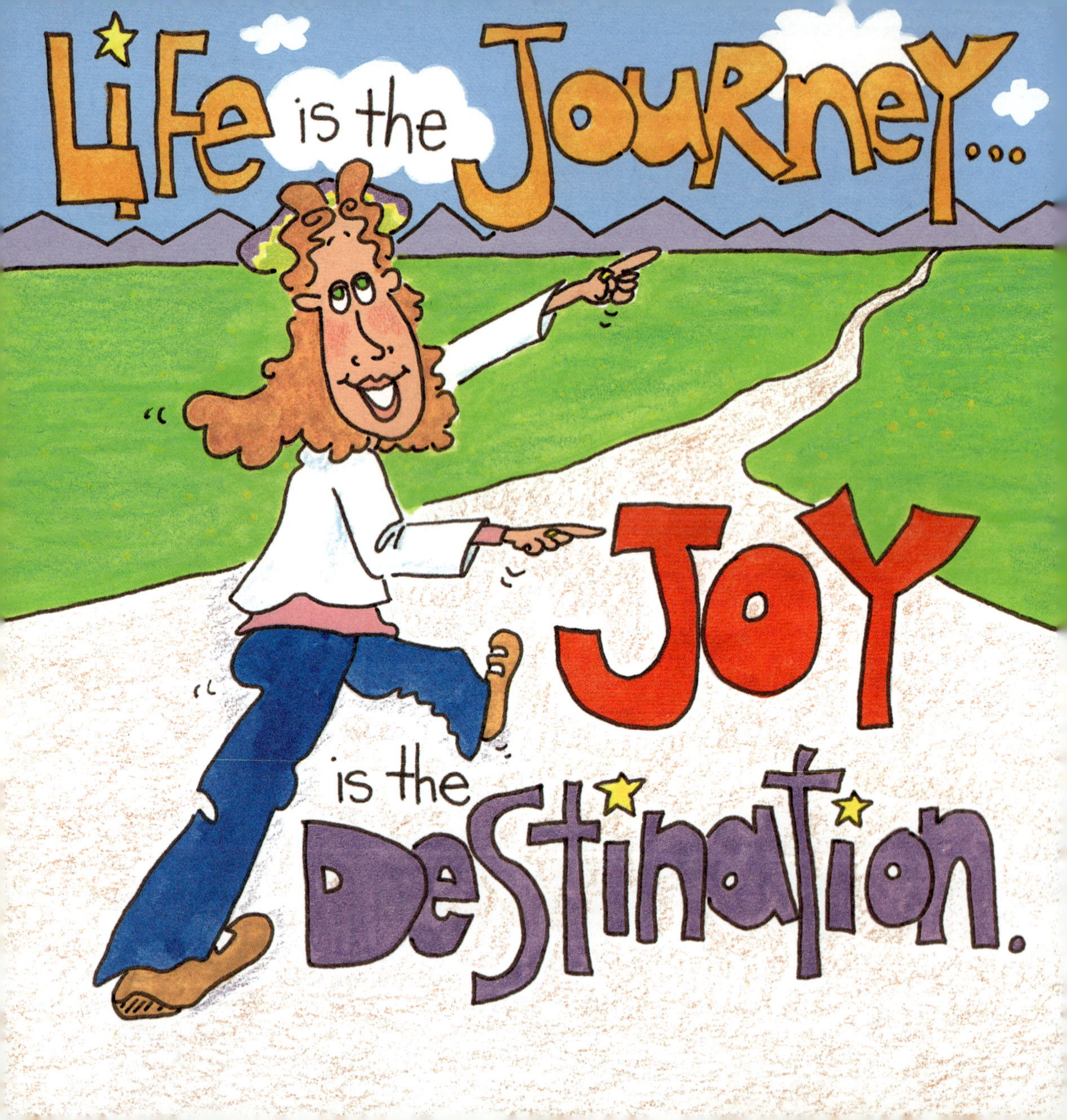
Life is the Journey...
Joy
is the Destination.

The Journey

A friend of mine and his mother were traveling to visit the university he was planning to attend. Mom, at the wheel, was contentedly driving along the USUAL ROUTE, the interstate... which is the way most people take for DIRECTNESS and for CERTAINTY. Mike, a very FREE-SPIRITED guy, suggested they turn off onto the next road going west.

Well, that meant **LEAVING THE OBVIOUS COURSE** and who knew where this unknown and untried road might lead?

The road was heading in the right direction, but it was certainly not the planned course. What was it then? An OPTION! The road was bound to be ROUGHER terrain than the smooth asphalt of the interstate, but that would PROVIDE INTEREST and Challenge. So why not simply Enjoy the SCENERY the side road offers? The Change of plan would definitely Create an Adventure!

And off they went, sitting up a little taller, EYES OPEN WIDE, setting a new rhythm. They had made a choice to step out of the tried and true and into new territory. They felt A NEW SENSE OF EXHILARATION!

And besides, with a four wheel drive vehicle... a VISA... a cell phone... Triple A... lots of water and blankets... and a bunch of food, THEY WERE VERY well-equipped."

Along the way, they saw incredible wildlife and scenery, things they might not have noticed or experienced had they stayed on the main road... things that provoked deeper **THOUGHT** and **INSPIRED** **CONVERSATION.**

Did it take them a little longer to get to their destination? **YES.**

Did they mind? **YES**, a little.

Did they enjoy the journey more? **YES**, they think so. AND THAT IS WHAT MATTERS.

Notice the Amazing things that surround you!

Taking Notice

ALL ALONG THE WAY of this journey through life are strewn bits and pieces of LESSONS and GIFTS. Sometimes we can see an order and a plan, while other times it feels like complete and utter chaos. The chaotic times are when I learned the BIG LESSONS, once I was able to crawl out from under the rubble.

There always seems to be a Light at the end of the tunnel... The light was a peaceful time, a time to SMILE and take a deep and SATISFYING BREATH, knowing IT HAS ALL BEEN VERY WORTHWHILE. The light brought a time to STOP and TAKE NOTICE.

Looking at the small things, the things that get passed over or taken for granted because they don't usually jump right out and scream "Look at me!" truly helps.

Noticing the moment and participating in

NOW... when we are doing that, we find clues to what it is we've been asking for help with... the answer to our

Prayers.

Wrapped up in the chaos, we can't see, or hear, or feel much other than the thing that has us all tied up. We miss **wonderful** things like **SUNRISES** and **SUNSETS**. We miss precious things like a child's **JOY**. Later we have regrets about moving so quickly through a particular period of the day, week, or year and wish we could do it over and

DO IT SLOWER.

But the moment is already gone forever.

Life is ours to cherish Every Day because, once the moment is gone, the GiFT of it is gone forever.

(Here is one of my favorite poems.)

If I had my Life to Live over...

I'd try to make more mistakes
next time.
I would RELAX. I would
LIMBER UP. I would
be a WHOLE LOT MORE
SILLY than I have
been this trip.

I know of very few things I would take seriously.

I would be Crazier.

I would be less hygienic.

I would CLIMB more mountains,

Swim more rivers

And watch more  Sunrises
and sunsets.

I would eat more ice cream
and less beans.
You see, I'm one of those people
who live sensibly and sanely,

HOUR BY HOUR
DAY BY DAY.

Oh, I've had my **moments**, and

If I had them to do over again,

I would Have

MORE

of them.

In fact, I'd try to have nothing else...

Just moments,

One after the other, instead of

Living so many years ahead,

So many miLes down the road.

I would go places traveling LIGHTER than I have.

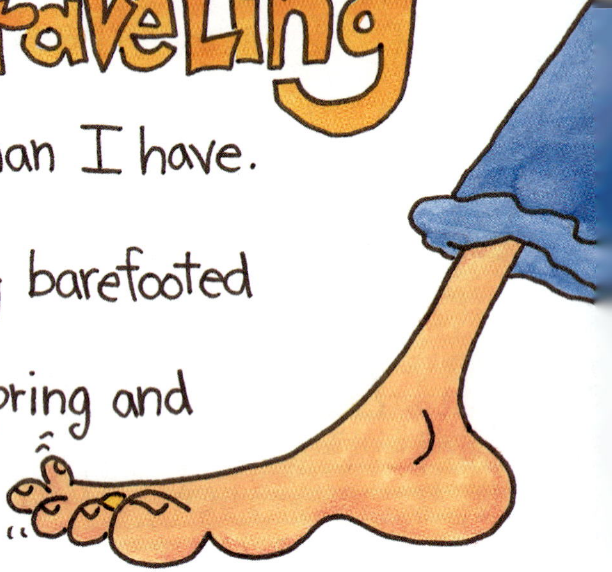

I would start going barefooted Earlier in the Spring and Later in the Fall...

I would play hooky more (shhh...) and I wouldn't make such good grades except by accident.

I would ride more merry-go-rounds.

I would definitely (for sure!) Pick More Daisies.

—anonymously written

Share A Smile!

Share A Smile

It seems to be our RESPONSIBILITY to TAKE CARE of EACH OTHER in some way. Otherwise, why on earth would there be SO MANY OF US? It doesn't have to be difficult, just as simple as giving a HEARTFELT SMILE and saying HELLO to someone.

If EVERYONE everywhere chose to DO SOMETHING TO MAKE ONE PERSON HAPPY each day, everyone in the whole world would

"SMILE"

at least once a day!

Smiling is healing.

We could even get to a point where we celebrate

Smile Day

FROM THE Heart like Valentine's Day.

If just one greeting card company picks up on the iDea, we'll all be celebrating a New Holiday!

On that day, SEND SMiLes OUT to Everyone you know and especially to those you don't know... you might find a new friend! Wear smiley-face shirts, hats, buttons. Decorate Yourself for SMiLE DAY like St. Patrick's Day and the wearin' of the green.

SMILE DAY could certainly be a MONTHLY EVENT – as I think about what time of the year is particularly needy, it feels like we could use this holiday

EVERY DAY.

There is some sadness going on in the world all the time, every moment... war within countries, war in the streets, war in the homes. A smile can be a GENTLE REMINDER PROMPTING US, nudging us to

REMEMBER the JOY we hold WiThin our souLs.

We can CHANGE OUR REALiTY by CHANGiNG OUR FOCUS, practicing and Dwelling on the PoSiTiVe aspects of life.

Learning to create joy and happiness by quieting the negative voice, shifting our attention to what is good in any given situation, will change what we perceive as reaLity.

As you THINK, so shall you BE.

Believe
Like it can be
No Other Way!

And so it will be no other way!

Thoughts become Dreams become Beliefs become REALITY.

Time and Patience

and Trust

Settling gently into the flow.

MOVING ALONG IN THE CURRENT

From one dream

to the next...

"Row, row, row your boat
Gently down the stream.
Merrily, merrily,
merrily, Merrily,

Life is but a Dream!

(New meaning to an old song...)

Sing the
Song
of your Soul!

THE SONG OF YOUR SOUL

What a great image, drawing in a big breath of air, opening wide, and letting out a full, loud and long bunch of notes and words that

"TELL THE STORY OF YOUR HEART."

The Song of your Soul is the truth of your SPIRIT, the pure and clear FEELING THAT IS ALL YOUR OWN.

To SPEAK YOUR TRUTH

is to give yourself a VERY GREAT GIFT OF CLARITY.

From a very young age, we have learned to alter our truth to gain approval, to save another person from discomfort, and to save ourself from having to LOOK at a part of our lives that makes us feel uncomfortable... a kind of self-imposed ignorance.

When I made my first attempts to get to the truth of my Being, I felt that I might as well have been digging to China through the center of the Earth with a spoon! It seemed nearly impossible to separate what my HEART had to say, from the voices I had let intertwine with my own.

There was the voice of my mother, my father, sister, brother, teachers, husband, children, and many other well-intentioned people.

And there was the voice of the media. I really didn't know how to "Begin to Decipher it all. What was mine and what was theirs and what might even be the same? One thing I did know was that it was important to sort through it and find my voice. At least I knew where to begin the search... in the place where the feeling of needing to find truth came from.

My Voice is the message
I speak
from my Heart,
the place of
Spirit...

Striking a Chord... Filling My Being with Light and the Song of My Soul!

Sometimes the voice of my soul, my HIGHEST SELF has a GREAT SENSE OF HUMOR, while other times it simply and clearly states its desire. It is never judgmental or unkind. Sometimes the voice is not a voice at all, but a Feeling... and usually it is both.

In the beginning of my journey through the center of the Earth with a spoon, I wondered...

"HOW WILL I BE ABLE TO TELL THE DIFFERENCE BETWEEN THE CLEAR GUIDANCE OF MY HIGHEST SELF, AND THE MIXED MESSAGES, ENCUMBERED BY OPINIONS OF OTHERS?"

The question is the answer. When the message is **CLEAR** and **UNENCUMBERED**, and I feel relaxed and WHOLE speaking the words, that is the VOICE of MY TRUTH.

It is pretty much that simple.

TRUTH is Simple and Clear!

What is the way to
The truth that's within?

A good start is to stop.

STOP to listen.
to see.
to feel.

Stop to sense what is there
Not so deep down inside...

EMBRACE TRUTH.

Once I found how to access my truth, I realized it is not possible to go back to my old ways of hiding without a very big feeLing of discomfort. I'm still learning after years of alteration. What is important is that I am clear and that I reflect that clarity in my actions. This whole way of being is as if I am

LIVING FROM THE INSIDE OUT...

...although I believe that SPIRIT is outside as well as inside... kind of INTEGRATED through the body. When the surface gets muddled, I take a big BREATH and go WITHIN to find the SOURCE of my HAPPINESS, the voice of my soul... the place where the simple truth resides and patiently waits for me to ACCESS IT.

Happiness is an Inside Job!

The "outside" job is to give voice to my spirit, teach it to sing, and use it for the highest good of the planet. Hmmmm... that must be why I'm here...

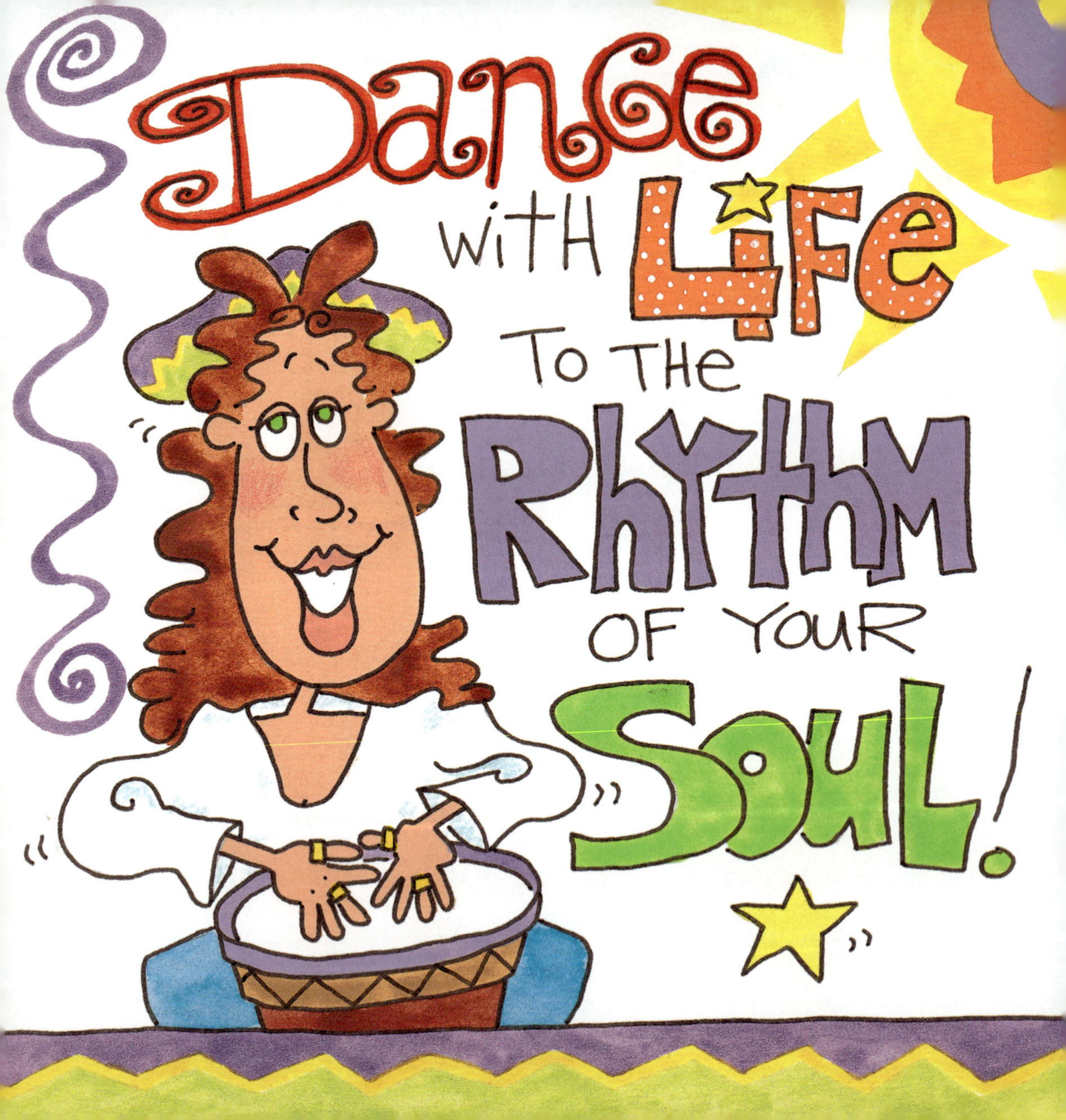
Dance with Life to the Rhythm of your Soul!

DANCE WITH LIFE!

One day, while checking out some **INSPIRATIONAL** sites on the internet, I came across two lines, written anonymously...

"DANCE LIKE NOBODY'S WATCHING. LOVE LIKE IT'S NEVER GOING TO HURT."

I wrote them down on a yellow sticky note and slapped it onto my computer monitor, figuring I would someday be able to use those words as

VERBAL REMEDIES.

I saw those words every day, either consciously or unconsciously as I worked at my computer. Weeks went by, and one day, for some reason I transferred the yellow sticky to the refrigerator in the kitchen where once a week fellow artists and good friends gathered for CLAY DAY.

CLAY DAY started out to be just that, a day to PLAY with clay. As things usually do, Clay Day evolved and became a DAY OF CREATIVE inspiration, a creative workshop that was great fun and FED OUR SOULS. It fueled our lives and our work. One of my friends, Karen, is an INCREDIBLE singer/songwriter who would sometimes bring her guitar and gift us with a song she had been **inspired** to write because of conversations from a previous CLAY DAY.

One CLAY DAY, with the stereo blasting out "Baby Love," I was inspired by Diana Ross and the **Spirit-Lifting** sound of the Supremes.

There I was JUST DANCING around the kitchen and the clay, while LYNN looked on in amusement. I caught the twinkLe in her eyes and her knowing SMILE and suddenly realized that I (normally extremely shy and self-conscious of every movement) had

LEARNED TO DANCE LIKE NOBODY'S WATCHING...

a great METAPHOR expressing my NEW ATTITUDE toward Life!

Dance
Like
Nobody
is
Watching!

I had proof that we can manifest that which we think about, consciously and unconsciously. Every day for a couple of months, these two phrases were in front of my eyes... unconscious affirmations of new ways I wanted to learn how to live. There I was living out the first line in its simplest definition, knowing I could apply this phrase to so many other pieces of my life.

Creating a new self-honesty and Truth, Learning to Love myself in the process.

Love like it's never going to hurt.

A LIGHT WENT ON. If I could ABSORB A PHRASE into my being by SIMPLY SEEING IT, what would happen if I CREATED and said a DAILY AFFIRMATION purposefully?

I had just started going through a separation and divorce. I needed STRENGTH I wasn't sure I had.

Every morning I ran around a lake in the park near my home. I decided to

CREATE AN AFFIRMATION

to say as I ran. Running took me out of my head and placed me determinedly in my body as I pushed myself to **COMPLETE** the circular path.

With **EACH STEP** I repeated

I am STRONG, Healthy, SMART, Kind and Beautiful!

Those words helped to pull me through a Time when I most needed to Believe they were True. They gave me Strength to move through each painful day.

The affirmation I say now is a bit different. When I first started saying it, I was having a difficult time finding consistent Joy and Peace, and who isn't in need of Abundance?

I wanted an affirmation to cover all my bases, so sharing my current personal affirmation with you (and inviting you to use it, too), this is what I am affirming now...

I am PEACEFUL...
I am JOYFUL...
I am ABUNDANT!

P.S. It's working!

CREATE YOUR OWN AFFIRMATIONS

Place them where you will see them everyday. See them and say them and believe them.

An Attitude of Gratitude

An Attitude of Gratitude

So you are OFF ON YOUR JOURNEY To FiNd Your DREAMS and live them. Along the way you will likely come across more than a few rocks in the road, maybe even some BIG BOULDERS, and probably lots of small, barely noticeable (unless you step on them) pebbles.

You may find that what seems to be a boulder to you is a pebble to someone else. Your **PERCEPTION** of what is before you **IS YOUR REALITY**, even though it may not be the same as the reality of others... it probably isn't. And **YOUR REALITY TODAY MAY NOT BE YOUR REALITY TOMORROW.**

A couple of years ago, during the transition of my divorce, I was pretty confused and very upset with what was happening in my youngest daughter's life. Her boyfriend's mother, Cindy, having lived through many more difficult life situations than I could understand at the time, tried to calm me down by telling me...

"This is just a Speedbump in Life."

I couldn't believe my ears.

"A SPEEDBUMP????! This is no SPEEDBUMP, it's a #!Z#ing rockslide in the middle of the road!!" I roared back at her very kind words. For me, it was a rockslide that I couldn't see around and for Cindy it was a speed bump to be

CAREFULLY NAVIGATED.

Same situation, two very different realities.

I have since learned to Trust,
and Look for the Lesson,
See the

If I look with my eyes and heart open, the silver lining appears and becomes a GOLDEN piece of INSPIRATION!

In learning this, there were many times when it was a struggle to find something positive in a situation I was not initially very happy about. *Little* BY *Little*, the effort became a WAY OF LIFE for me.

Practice Positive

I developed the ability to

Scout out the

LIGHT

in the dark through an

ATTITUDE

of GRATITUDE...

...for whatever was placed in my view, knowing it was bringing me a LESSON I needed to learn. My beloved daughter's difficulties led her to GREATER WISDOM and us to an even closer relationship. Cindy, WISE WOMAN, knew that anything my daughter was experiencing could be TURNED INTO GOLD!

An Attitude of Gratitude
Illuminates the Soul.

There are days when I occasionally have trouble **FINDING THE LIGHT**. Those are the days when I would like to pull the covers up over my head and **WAKE UP** when the trouble has gone far away. But the truth is that whatever is bothering me isn't going to run away because it can't see me under the

BLANKET.

In fact, it probably hangs out at the edge of the bed waiting for my head to appear.

So I have learned to

MUSTER UP THE COURAGE

to **LOOK** the mess square in the face,

ACKNOWLEDGE it for what it is trying to

TEACH ME and...

...Go about Finding

THE LIGHT!

With an extra ounce (or maybe POUND) of effort, it always SURFACES sooner or later.

Finding a POSITIVE OUTLOOK is well worth the effort. It has connected me to the JOY and ABUNDANCE OF THE UNIVERSE, creating a feeling of SOARING! The picture that comes to my mind is Flying through the air with a Smile on my face and a "GLOW" in my heart!

Let Your Spirit

SOAR

Like the **wind**.

FLY over and through

Fields of flowers,
Leaves and branches,
Blades of grass!

Let Your Spirit

Flow

With the Earth...

Call on the Clouds.

Visit the MOON.

DISCOVER a star!

Find your **SOUL**

Looking out from within.

LET YOUR SPIRIT
SOAR!

WE ARE
ONE!

We Are ONE!

I have shared some of my journey thus far in the HOPE that something I have written will resonate somewhere in you and inspire you to STEP OUT of your own "safe" place, get uncomfortable, and stumble onto a Journey toward a dream you have held in your heart. All along my own way I have met people whose stories have inspired and given me strength.

We are not so different as it might seem at a quick glance. At the very core of us,

We Are the Same.

I am eternally **grateful** to those earthly and **Heavenly** beings who **Stand by me** while I walk about on this exhilarating **Spiritual Path** and I **Salute** my fellow travelers,

RECOGNIZING YOU, knowing WE ARE PART OF THE UNIVERSAL WHOLE.

NaMasté

Namasté is Sanskrit and means

"I honor the place in you where we are one."

At the highest level of our existence, our spirits walk together as one.

First and foremost, my job is to take care of myself, so that job does not fall to others. Once I take on that responsibility, dare to dream, and begin the steps to live that dream, I give myself the power and energy to give back to the whole.

Acknowledge the oneness within another person's being.

Let your spirit shine through!

Make a difference every day!

LET YOUR SPIRIT SHINE!

Dare to Dream.
Dare to Dream **HUGE!**
Dream with Conviction.
Believe in Your ability
To make Your wildest dreams
Come **True!**
The **Power** is within You.

I wish you well on your journey. Remember that whatever bumps or curves lie ahead are merely that... speedbumps in the road of life.

May you live your wildest dreams of endless possibilities!

Peace and 

Love...

Bio of the Artist...

Breah Parker is an artist living in beautiful Black Mountain, North Carolina. She has traveled many paths in the journey to her life's work, including a corporate career, marriage (and divorce), motherhood, friendship, soul-searching and professional endeavors in art direction and licensing. All the while her artistic nature has called to her. She created cartoon creation Lorelie as a light-hearted spirit to carry her message, encouraging all women to honor, nurture, and love themselves, while living lives of fulfillment and wonder.

An Artist Draws on the Spirit within.